"BJP Unboxed: The Story of India's Political Powerhouse"

BJP Unboxed: The Story of India's Political Powerhouse

Ankush vig

Published by Ankush vig, 2024.

BJP UNBOXED: THE STORY OF INDIA'S POLITICAL POWERHOUSE

First edition. January 29, 2024.

Copyright © 2024 Ankush vig.

ISBN: 979-8224477227

Written by Ankush vig.

Table of Contents

Table of Contents

Introduction

Social Welfare Initiatives

11.3 Challenges and Opportunities: Navigating Complexities for Inclusive Growth

<u>**2024 Elections Predictions**</u>

12.1 Current Political Landscape
12.2 BJP's Strengths and Potential Challenges
12.3 Challenges and Opportunities
12.4 Public Perception and Voter Sentiment
12.5 The Way Forward

<u>**Challenges and Opportunities Ahead**</u>

13.1 Issues to Address
13.2 Opportunities for Growth

<u>**Conclusion**</u>

14.1 Summarising the BJP's Journey
14.2 Reflections on India's Political Future

<u>**Introduction:**</u>

As the sun set on the eve of India's independence in 1947, a new nation emerged from the shadows of colonial rule, laden with aspirations and dreams of progress. Little did the founding leaders anticipate the intricacies and challenges that would define the trajectory of Indian politics over the decades to come. In this nuanced exploration, we embark on a comprehensive journey through the pages of India's political history, focusing on the Bharatiya Janata Party (BJP), a political force that has significantly shaped the nation's narrative from its inception to the anticipated 2024 elections.

<u>**1.1 Background: A Political Odyssey Unveiled**</u>

The genesis of the BJP can be traced back to 1980, a pivotal moment in India's political landscape. The party emerged from the womb of the

Rashtriya Swayamsevak Sangh (RSS), a socio-cultural organisation that espoused the principles of cultural nationalism. Founded with the objective of championing the cause of Hindutva and providing a political platform for those who identified with this ideology, the BJP embarked on a journey that would see it evolve into a dominant force in Indian politics.

Through the lens of this book, we delve into the foundational principles that shaped the BJP, exploring its early leaders' roles, particularly the influential Atal Bihari Vajpayee and L.K. Advani, who steered the party through its formative years.

1.2 Objective of the Book: Unraveling the BJP Tapestry

The primary objective of "BJP Unboxed: The Story of India's Political Powerhouse" is to provide readers with a panoramic view of the BJP's evolution. Through meticulous research and analysis, this book aims to present a comprehensive narrative that goes beyond mere political documentation. Here are the key objectives that guide this exploration:

- **Historical Contextualization**: To place the BJP within the broader historical context of post-independence India, analyzing the socio-political milieu that influenced its formation and growth. By understanding the historical underpinnings, readers can appreciate the factors that propelled the BJP onto the national stage.

- **Leadership Exploration**: To unravel the distinctive leadership styles of key figures like Atal Bihari Vajpayee and L.K. Advani, exploring how their ideologies and strategies shaped the party. Through this exploration, readers gain insights into the leadership dynamics that propelled the BJP from a regional entity to a national force.

- **Policy Examination**: To dissect the policies championed by the BJP, from economic reforms to social welfare initiatives. By examining the rationale behind decisions like the abrogation of Article 370 and the implementation of the Citizenship Amendment Act (CAA), readers gain an understanding of the BJP's governance philosophy.

- **Vision for India:** To elucidate the BJP's vision for India, focusing on its economic goals, infrastructure development initiatives, and its approach to national security. This objective seeks to illuminate the party's broader aspirations and its role in steering India towards progress.

- **Inclusive Governance**: To highlight the BJP's efforts in inclusive governance, specifically its outreach programs in South India and the North East. The book examines the party's initiatives to provide education to Muslims, emphasizing its commitment to national unity and social harmony.

- **Looking Ahead to 2024:** To offer informed predictions and analysis of the political landscape leading up to the 2024 elections. This objective involves assessing the current state of Indian politics, understanding the challenges and opportunities for the BJP, and speculating on the party's potential future trajectory.

- **Challenges and Opportunities**: To critically examine the challenges faced by the BJP and identify potential opportunities for growth. By acknowledging areas that need attention, the book aims to contribute to a constructive dialogue on India's political future.

- In essence, "BJP Unveiled" seeks to unravel the layers of India's political journey, with the BJP as the focal point. It is not just a documentation of political events; rather, it is an exploration of the ideologies, decisions, and leaders that have steered the ship of the world's largest democracy through decades of change. As we embark on this journey through the BJP's history, the objective is to provide readers with a nuanced understanding, fostering an appreciation for the complexities that define India's political landscape.

Chapter 2: Founding Principles and Early Leaders

In the crucible of India's post-independence era, marked by the fervour of nation-building and the forging of a democratic identity, the Bharatiya Janata Party (BJP) emerged as a political force in 1980. The genesis of the party can be traced back to the socio-cultural roots of the Rashtriya Swayamsevak Sangh (RSS), which sought to imbue the political landscape with the principles of cultural nationalism and Hindutva. This chapter endeavors to unravel the foundational principles that shaped the BJP during its formative years, exploring the early leaders who played instrumental roles in crafting the party's identity.

2.1 Emergence of the BJP:

The backdrop against which the BJP came into existence was one of political flux and ideological evolution. The aftermath of the Emergency (1975-1977) and the subsequent Janata Party government marked a transformative period in Indian politics. The Janata Party, an amalgamation of opposition forces, held power at the centre. However, ideological differences within the coalition led to its eventual collapse.

In this political vacuum, the precursor to the BJP, the Bharatiya Jana Sangh (BJS), emerged. The BJS, itself a product of a merger between the Janata Party and the RSS, laid the groundwork for the BJP's formation. The BJS was dissolved in 1980, making way for the birth of the Bharatiya Janata Party. The new entity was driven by a vision that sought to provide a political platform for those who identified with the cultural and ideological ethos of Hindutva.

2.2 Role of Atal Bihari Vajpayee and L.K. Advani:

The early years of the BJP were characterised by the dynamic leadership of Atal Bihari Vajpayee and L.K. Advani. Atal Bihari Vajpayee, a charismatic orator and seasoned politician, served as the party's first president. His leadership style combined statesmanship with a pragmatic approach to politics. Vajpayee's ability to articulate the party's vision and engage with a diverse political landscape played a pivotal role in establishing the BJP as a credible political force.

L.K. Advani, often regarded as the architect of the BJP's growth, brought strategic acumen and organisational skills to the fore. His tenure as the party's president saw the BJP making significant inroads in national politics. The Rath Yatra in 1990, led by Advani, advocating the construction of the Ram Mandir in Ayodhya, catapulted the party into the national consciousness and became a defining moment in its trajectory.

Together, Vajpayee and Advani shaped the BJP's early identity, steering it through the challenges of coalition politics and contributing to its growth. Their partnership laid the foundation for the BJP's electoral success and marked a departure from the fringe to the mainstream of Indian politics.

2.3 Ideological Bedrock:

At the ideological core of the BJP was the concept of Hindutva, a term coined by Vinayak Damodar Savarkar in the early 20th century. The BJP, while advocating for the interests of Hindus, maintained that Hindutva was not synonymous with anti-minority sentiments. Instead, it emphasised cultural nationalism, asserting that all Indian citizens, irrespective of their religious affiliations, were inheritors of the nation's ancient civilization.

The party's commitment to Hindutva was enshrined in its manifesto, which sought to uphold the cultural and spiritual heritage of India. The BJP envisioned a nation that celebrated its diversity while preserving a common cultural thread that bound its people together.

2.4 Challenges and Evolution:

The early years of the BJP were not without challenges. The party grappled with the task of balancing its cultural and ideological moorings with the need to appeal to a diverse and secular electorate. The demolition of the Babri Masjid in Ayodhya in 1992, a contentious event linked to the Ram Janmabhoomi-Babri Masjid dispute, presented a significant challenge to the BJP's image and tested its commitment to the principles of pluralism. However, the BJP's resilience in the face of challenges marked a defining characteristic of the party's early years. The ability to adapt and evolve in response to changing political landscapes became a hallmark of the BJP's approach.

2.5 Legacy of Founding Principles:

The founding principles of the BJP, rooted in cultural nationalism and Hindutva, have left an indelible mark on Indian politics. While the party faced criticisms for its ideological stance, it also succeeded in providing a political platform for a significant section of the population that identified with its vision.

The legacy of Atal Bihari Vajpayee and L.K. Advani, the founding leader who nurtured the party during its nascent years, continues to influence the BJP's identity. The party's journey from the margins to the mainstream is a testament to the enduring impact of its founding principles and the leadership that steered it through its formative phase.

Chapter 3: Modi and Yogi: Transformative Leadership in the BJP's Evolution

In the annals of the Bharatiya Janata Party's (BJP) history, two leaders have played pivotal roles in transforming the party's fortunes and reshaping the political landscape of India's states. Narendra Modi, with his charismatic and dynamic leadership, has propelled the BJP from being a regional force to a central powerhouse. Similarly, Yogi Adityanath, through his governance in Uttar Pradesh (UP), has orchestrated a paradigm shift, turning the state from a bastion of lawlessness to a thriving business hub marked by enhanced safety and development.

3.1 Narendra Modi: A National Icon

As Narendra Modi assumed office as the Prime Minister of India in 2014, he brought with him a vision that extended beyond regional politics. His leadership style, characterized by decisiveness and a focus on development, resonated with a diverse national electorate. Modi's transformative governance in the state of Gujarat had already garnered attention, and as he assumed the mantle of the country's leadership, the BJP underwent a metamorphosis into a truly national party.

Modi's vision for India was predicated on the principles of economic growth, infrastructure development, and social inclusion. His flagship initiatives, such as 'Make in India,' 'Swachh Bharat Abhiyan,' and 'Pradhan Mantri Jan Dhan Yojana,' exemplified his commitment to inclusive development. The successful implementation of the Goods and Services Tax (GST) and the demonetization drive were bold moves aimed at reshaping India's economic landscape.

What set Modi apart was his ability to communicate effectively with the masses. The 'Mann Ki Baat' radio program and the adept use of social media platforms allowed him to connect directly with the citizens, transcending regional and linguistic barriers. The BJP, under Modi's leadership, ceased to be confined to a particular region; it became a symbol of national aspirations and transformative governance.

3.2 Modi's Vision Acceptance Across States:

One of the remarkable aspects of Narendra Modi's leadership has been the acceptance of his vision across diverse states and cultures. While Gujarat had been the laboratory for his governance experiments, Modi successfully translated his vision into policies that resonated with the aspirations of people from Jammu and Kashmir to Tamil Nadu.

States like Maharashtra, Haryana, and Assam witnessed significant electoral victories for the BJP, signaling the party's expanding footprint under Modi's leadership. The 'Modi wave' became a political phenomenon, reflecting a broader acceptance of his developmental agenda and a departure from traditional caste and regional politics.

The implementation of central schemes, such as 'Ujjwala Yojana' providing LPG connections to rural households and 'Pradhan Mantri Awas Yojana' for affordable housing, showcased a commitment to improving the lives of people across states. Modi's emphasis on cooperative federalism and collaborative governance with states contributed to a sense of national cohesion.

3.3 Yogi Adityanath: Transforming Uttar Pradesh

In Uttar Pradesh, India's most populous state, Yogi Adityanath assumed the chief ministerial office in 2017. His appointment marked a departure from conventional politics, and Yogi's governance swiftly targeted deep-seated issues that had plagued the state for years.

The 'Uttar Pradesh Model of Development' under Yogi Adityanath prioritised law and order, infrastructure, and economic growth. In a state that had been synonymous with political patronage, criminality, and a lack of business-friendly policies, Yogi initiated a dramatic turnaround.

3.4 Restoring Law and Order:

One of the foremost challenges Yogi Adityanath confronted was the pervasive lawlessness that had earned Uttar Pradesh the moniker of being a hub of criminal activities. His government adopted a zero-tolerance approach to crime and initiated police reforms. The crackdown on organized crime, coupled with swift and transparent justice delivery, sent a strong message that UP was no longer a haven for criminal elements.

The 'Anti-Romeo' squads aimed at curbing eve-teasing, and the stringent action against illegal sand mining underscored the administration's commitment to ensuring safety and adherence to the rule of law. Yogi's focus on law and order not only enhanced the state's security but also contributed to creating an environment conducive to business and investment.

3.5 Business Hub and Development Initiatives:

Yogi Adityanath's vision for UP extended beyond curbing crime; it encompassed transforming the state into an attractive destination for business and investment. The 'One District, One Product' (ODOP) scheme aimed at promoting traditional industries and crafts, providing economic opportunities at the grassroots level.

The express intent to develop infrastructure, including the construction of the Purvanchal Expressway, the Bundelkhand Expressway, and the defense corridor, underscored Yogi's commitment to catalyzing economic growth. These projects not only improved connectivity within the state but also positioned UP as an investment-friendly destination.

3.6 Socio-Economic and Cultural Initiatives:

In addition to economic reforms, Yogi Adityanath's administration focused on socio-economic initiatives. The 'Namami Gange' project aimed at cleaning and revitalizing the Ganges, a river of immense cultural and religious significance in the state. Efforts to improve healthcare infrastructure, such as the establishment of AIIMS in Gorakhpur, contributed to enhancing the overall quality of life.

Yogi's emphasis on cultural preservation was evident in his support for the Kumbh Mela, a massive religious gathering, and his proactive stance on the Ayodhya issue. The state's cultural heritage became a key aspect of Yogi's governance, fostering a sense of pride and identity among its residents.

3.7 Environmental and Infrastructure Development:

Environmental sustainability was another facet of Yogi Adityanath's vision for UP. Initiatives such as the 'Green UP, Clean UP' campaign aimed at environmental conservation, afforestation, and sustainable development. The focus on renewable energy projects aligned with a broader commitment to balance developmental goals with environmental responsibility.

The emphasis on improving healthcare infrastructure, the successful management of the COVID-19 crisis, and the distribution of free ration during the pandemic demonstrated Yogi's proactive and people-centric governance.

3.8 Yogi's Popularity and National Influence:

Similar to Narendra Modi's impact on national politics, Yogi Adityanath's popularity transcended the boundaries of Uttar Pradesh. His style of governance and commitment to development found resonance with a wider audience. The perception of UP as a state synonymous with crime and administrative inertia underwent a substantial transformation under Yogi's leadership.

Yogi Adityanath's influence extended beyond UP, with his voice carrying weight in national conversations. His administrative approach, particularly in dealing with the COVID-19 pandemic, garnered attention and admiration.

3.9 Lessons from Modi and Yogi:

The leadership of Narendra Modi and Yogi Adityanath provides valuable insights into transformative governance. Their ability to articulate a vision, coupled with decisive action and a focus on development, has not only changed the fortunes of their respective states but has also reshaped the BJP into a truly national party.

The Modi-Yogi model underscores the significance of visionary leadership in navigating complex challenges and steering a party or state towards progress. The acceptance of their governance models across states reflects a broader shift in Indian politics, emphasizing development, inclusivity, and a departure from traditional, identity-based politics.

Chapter 4: Vision for India

As the Bharatiya Janata Party (BJP) emerged on India's political stage, it brought with it a vision that transcended the conventional paradigms of governance. This chapter delves into the BJP's vision for India, examining its economic goals, commitment to self-reliance, and its approach to infrastructure development, national security, and cultural preservation. It's a narrative that unfolds against the backdrop of a nation aspiring to not only grow economically but to redefine its global identity.

4.1 Economic Reforms and Self-Reliance:

Central to the BJP's vision for India was an economic blueprint that aimed not just for growth, but for transformative change. The party championed economic reforms that fostered a business-friendly environment, encouraged entrepreneurship, and sought to propel India into the league of major global economies.

The concept of self-reliance, articulated as "Atmanirbhar Bharat," became a rallying point for the BJP. It represented a paradigm shift in India's economic philosophy, emphasizing reducing dependence on imports and promoting indigenous industries. This vision gained prominence in the wake of global challenges, such as the COVID-19 pandemic, underscoring the importance of self-sufficiency in critical sectors.

4.2 Infrastructure Development Initiatives:

A critical pillar of the BJP's vision was the transformation of India's infrastructure. The Pradhan Mantri Gram Sadak Yojana (PMGSY) aimed at connecting rural areas with all-weather roads, fostering economic development in regions that were historically marginalized. Simultaneously, the Bharatmala Pariyojana focused on the development of a robust network of national highways, enhancing connectivity and facilitating smoother transportation of goods and people.

Beyond roads, the BJP's vision extended to railways, with the introduction of the Dedicated Freight Corridor (DFC) to improve freight transportation efficiency. Ambitious high-speed rail projects, including the Mumbai-Ahmedabad Bullet Train, reflected a commitment to modernizing rail travel and connecting major urban centers.

The aviation sector underwent a significant facelift with the UDAN (Ude Desh ka Aam Naagrik) scheme, enhancing regional connectivity by developing underserved and unserved airports. This comprehensive approach to infrastructure development reflected the BJP's commitment to creating a well-connected, modern India.

4.3 National Security Priorities:

National security has consistently been at the forefront of the BJP's vision. The party's commitment to a strong defense apparatus was underscored by its resolute stance against terrorism. The surgical strikes conducted in response to the Uri and Pulwama attacks served as a testament to India's commitment to safeguarding its borders and responding decisively to security threats.

The BJP's vision for national security extended beyond reactive measures. The emphasis on strengthening border infrastructure, modernizing the armed forces, and investing in defense capabilities reflected a proactive approach to safeguarding India's sovereignty. The doctrine of 'Integrated Defense' sought to synergize the capabilities of the army, navy, and air force, ensuring a holistic and effective response to evolving security challenges.

4.4 Cultural Preservation and Promotion:

While economic growth and national security were pivotal, the BJP's vision for India encompassed the preservation and promotion of its rich cultural heritage. The promotion of yoga on the global stage, recognition and celebration of Indian festivals at the national level, and efforts to revive traditional art forms reflected the party's commitment to cultural rejuvenation.

The construction of the Ram Mandir in Ayodhya, a long-standing and contentious issue, was a significant milestone in the BJP's vision for cultural preservation. It aimed to reconcile historical grievances while symbolizing a commitment to India's cultural continuity.

4.5 Social and Economic Inclusion:

Integral to the BJP's vision was the principle of inclusive development. The party sought to bridge social and economic gaps by implementing policies that uplifted the marginalized and vulnerable sections of society. The Pradhan Mantri Jan Dhan Yojana aimed at financial inclusion, providing banking facilities to the unbanked. Similarly, the Pradhan Mantri Jan Arogya Yojana (Ayushman Bharat) aimed at making quality healthcare accessible to all, especially the economically weaker sections.

In the realm of education, initiatives like the Skill India Mission and the Atal Innovation Mission aimed to empower the youth with skills and foster innovation. The vision for social and economic inclusion reflected the BJP's commitment to ensuring that the benefits of progress reached every stratum of society.

4.6 Technological Advancements and Digital India:

Recognizing the transformative potential of technology, the BJP led the Digital India campaign. This ambitious initiative aimed to bridge the digital divide, bring technology to the grassroots, and transform India into a digitally empowered society. E-governance initiatives, the push for digital payments, and the expansion of internet connectivity were central to the BJP's vision for a tech-savvy and connected nation.

4.7 Environmental Sustainability:

The BJP's vision for India also acknowledged the imperative of environmental sustainability. Initiatives such as Swachh Bharat Abhiyan focused on cleanliness and sanitation, contributing to a healthier and more sustainable environment. The emphasis on renewable energy, afforestation, and initiatives like the Namami Gange project underscored the party's commitment to balancing developmental goals with environmental conservation.

The BJP's vision for India is a comprehensive tapestry that weaves together economic growth, national security, cultural preservation, social inclusion, technological advancement, and environmental sustainability. It is a vision that embraces the complexities of a diverse nation, seeking not just progress but a holistic and inclusive development that resonates with the spirit of a resurgent India.

Chapter 5: Defence and Strong Stance Against Terrorism

In the intricate dance of geopolitics and national security, the Bharatiya Janata Party (BJP) has stood firm, advocating a robust defence policy and an unwavering stance against terrorism. This chapter delves into the party's priorities in safeguarding India's borders, its responses to acts of terrorism, and the strategic vision that underpins its defence doctrine.

5.1 National Security Priorities:

National security lies at the heart of the BJP's governance philosophy. The party has consistently emphasised the need for a strong and capable defense apparatus to safeguard the sovereignty and integrity of the nation. The evolving geopolitical landscape, coupled with persistent threats along India's borders, has shaped the BJP's priorities in ensuring the country's security.

The modernization of the armed forces, investment in defense capabilities, and the development of strategic infrastructure have been central to the BJP's national security agenda. The party recognizes that a secure and stable environment is a prerequisite for sustained economic growth and the overall well-being of its citizens.

5.2 Surgical Strikes and Responses to Terrorism:

The BJP's response to acts of terrorism has been characterized by a proactive and resolute approach. The surgical strikes conducted in 2016 and 2019 were watershed moments that signalled a departure from a policy of restraint to one of measured retaliation. In 2016, following the Uri terrorist attack, and in 2019, after the Pulwama attack, India's armed forces carried out precise and targeted operations across the Line of Control (LoC), neutralising terrorist launch pads.

These surgical strikes were not merely military actions; they were bold statements that affirmed India's determination to protect its citizens and respond decisively to provocations. The BJP, under the leadership of Prime Minister Narendra Modi, sent a clear message to both state and non-state actors that India would not hesitate to defend itself against acts of terrorism.

5.3 Integrated Defense Doctrine:

The BJP's defense doctrine is anchored in the concept of integrated defense, acknowledging the need for a coordinated and synergized approach across all branches of the armed forces. The party has advocated for the modernization of the military, ensuring that it is equipped with state-of-the-art technology and capabilities to respond effectively to contemporary security challenges.

The emphasis on integrated defense involves fostering greater coordination and interoperability between the army, navy, and air force. This holistic approach seeks to leverage the strengths of each branch to enhance the overall effectiveness of India's defense capabilities. The creation of the post of Chief of Defense Staff (CDS) in 2019 is a significant step towards achieving this integration.

5.4 Countering Cross-Border Terrorism:

The BJP has consistently taken a strong stance against cross-border terrorism, particularly emanating from Pakistan. The party argues that terrorism and talks cannot go hand in hand, asserting that meaningful dialogue can only occur in an environment free from the shadow of violence and terror. The issue of Pakistan-sponsored terrorism, particularly in the context of the Kashmir conflict, has been a focal point of India's diplomatic efforts.

The BJP's approach involves both diplomatic initiatives to isolate state sponsors of terrorism and military responses to neutralize terrorist threats. The abrogation of Article 370 in Jammu and Kashmir in 2019, a longstanding demand of the BJP, was seen as a move to integrate the region more closely with the rest of the country and address security concerns.

5.5 Border Infrastructure Development:

Recognizing the importance of robust border infrastructure in securing the nation's borders, the BJP has undertaken initiatives to enhance connectivity and logistics along border areas. The construction of roads, bridges, and strategic infrastructure along the Line of Actual Control (LAC) with China and the LoC with Pakistan is a crucial aspect of the party's defense strategy.

Improved border infrastructure not only facilitates swift mobilization of troops but also enhances the accessibility of remote areas, contributing to the overall development of border regions. The Darbuk-Shyok-Daulat Beg Oldi (DSDBO) road in Ladakh and the Atal Tunnel in Himachal Pradesh are examples of strategic projects aimed at strengthening India's defense capabilities.

5.6 Nuclear Doctrine and Deterrence:

The BJP has upheld a policy of credible minimum deterrence in the realm of nuclear weapons. India's nuclear doctrine, as articulated by the BJP, emphasizes a no-first-use posture while retaining the flexibility to respond effectively to nuclear aggression. The party advocates for maintaining a robust and credible nuclear deterrent to safeguard national security interests.

The BJP's approach to nuclear weapons is rooted in the belief that they serve as a deterrent, preventing potential adversaries from contemplating nuclear aggression. The party underscores the importance of responsible nuclear behavior and seeks to contribute to global efforts towards nuclear disarmament and non-proliferation.

5.7 Challenges and Responses:

While the BJP's defense and security policies have seen significant successes, challenges persist. The evolving nature of asymmetric threats, cyber warfare, and the need for continuous technological upgrades pose ongoing challenges. The party recognizes the imperative of adapting to new security paradigms and investing in cutting-edge technologies to stay ahead of potential threats.

Moreover, the BJP has grappled with the intricacies of handling insurgency and internal security challenges, particularly in regions affected by Left-Wing Extremism (LWE) and militancy. Balancing the need for a strong response with efforts towards addressing the root causes of these challenges remains an ongoing priority.

5.8 Global Diplomacy and Defense Alliances:

The BJP has actively engaged in global diplomacy to strengthen defense alliances and garner support for India's security concerns. Building partnerships with like-minded nations, participating in joint military exercises, and collaborating on defense research and technology have been integral to the party's approach.

Strategic partnerships with countries such as the United States, Israel, and Russia have bolstered India's defense capabilities through the acquisition of advanced technology, joint training programs, and intelligence-sharing arrangements. The BJP's diplomatic efforts aim to create a conducive international environment that supports India's national security interests.

5.9 The Way Forward:

The BJP's defense and security policies underscore the party's commitment to safeguarding India's interests in a volatile global environment. The emphasis on a strong defense apparatus, integrated defense doctrine, and decisive responses to terrorism reflects a strategic vision that prioritizes the nation's security.

As India navigates a complex geopolitical landscape, the challenges and opportunities in the realm of defense and security continue to evolve. The BJP's approach, marked by proactive measures, technological advancements, and global engagement, is geared towards ensuring that India not only defends its borders but also plays a constructive role in shaping regional and global security dynamics. The party's commitment to a strong defense and an unwavering stance against terrorism remains central to its vision for a secure and prosperous India.

Chapter 6: Historical Issues - Article 370 to Ram Mandir

In the intricate tapestry of India's political history, certain issues have been touchstones, shaping the socio-political landscape and evoking passionate debates. This chapter explores two such historical issues that have left an indelible mark on the nation's consciousness: the abrogation of Article 370 and the construction of the Ram Mandir in Ayodhya.

6.1 Article 370: A Historical Legacy Unraveled

The genesis of Article 370 can be traced back to the complex circumstances surrounding the accession of the princely state of Jammu and Kashmir to the newly formed Union of India in 1947. Drafted as a temporary provision within the Indian Constitution, Article 370 granted special autonomy to Jammu and Kashmir, allowing the state to have its own constitution and decision-making powers in all matters except defense, communications, and foreign affairs.

Over the years, Article 370 became a symbol of the unique relationship between the Indian Union and Jammu and Kashmir. However, it also fueled contentious debates, with critics arguing that the special status accorded to the state hindered its integration into the national mainstream and perpetuated a separate identity.

The BJP, historically critical of Article 370, viewed it as a hurdle to the full integration of Jammu and Kashmir into the Indian Union. The party's commitment to national unity and its vision of a uniform legal and political framework across all states led to a sustained demand for the abrogation of Article 370.

The turning point came on August 5, 2019, when the BJP-led government, under Prime Minister Narendra Modi, took the bold step of abrogating Article 370 and bifurcating the state into two Union Territories - Jammu & Kashmir and Ladakh. The move sparked a range of reactions, from vehement support to intense opposition, and reshaped the political and constitutional landscape of the region.

The abrogation of Article 370 was not merely a legal maneuver; it was a historical and political recalibration, reflecting the BJP's commitment to a more unified and integrated India. The move sought to dismantle historical intricacies and assert a sense of oneness within the diverse fabric of the nation.

6.2 Ram Mandir: A Symbolic Resolution

The Ayodhya dispute, rooted in centuries of historical and religious complexities, centred around the Babri Masjid and the belief that it was built on the birthplace of Lord Ram. The issue simmered for decades, leading to communal tensions and, eventually, the demolition of the Babri Masjid in 1992.

The BJP, since its inception, had been vocal about its commitment to the construction of a Ram Mandir at the disputed site. The party, rooted in the ideology of Hindutva, saw the Ayodhya issue as not just a legal dispute but as a matter of cultural and religious identity. The call for the construction of the Ram Mandir resonated with a significant section of its voter base, and it became a rallying point for the party.

The protracted legal battles, spanning decades and involving various stakeholders, culminated in a historic judgement by the Supreme Court of India in November 2019. The court's verdict recognized the legitimacy of the Hindu claim to the disputed site and directed the allocation of alternate land for the construction of a mosque.

The subsequent groundbreaking ceremony for the construction of the Ram Mandir in Ayodhya, attended by Prime Minister Narendra Modi, marked the realization of a long-cherished dream for many within the BJP and its supporters. The event was not just about the construction of a physical structure; it symbolized the triumph of cultural aspirations and the end of a protracted chapter in India's history.

6.3 BJP's Approach to Historical Issues:

The BJP's approach to historical issues like Article 370 and the Ayodhya dispute reflects a commitment to address longstanding challenges and reshape the narrative of Indian identity. The party's leaders, including Prime Minister Narendra Modi and influential figures like L.K. Advani played instrumental roles in steering the party's stance on these issues.

In the case of Article 370, the BJP's approach was rooted in the belief that the special autonomy granted to Jammu and Kashmir had perpetrated a sense of separateness. The party argued that the abrogation of Article 370 was not just a legal amendment but a historical correction, aligning the state more closely with the rest of the nation.

Similarly, the BJP's approach to the Ayodhya issue reflected a commitment to cultural and religious identity. The party maintained that the construction of the Ram Mandir was not an act of erasure but a restoration of a historical and spiritual heritage. The legal resolution of the dispute through the Supreme Court's verdict sought to provide closure to a longstanding issue while emphasizing the principles of justice and inclusivity.

6.4 Controversies and Criticisms:

The decisions surrounding Article 370 and the construction of the Ram Mandir were not without controversies and criticisms. The abrogation of Article 370 stirred international concerns and drew criticism from some quarters, questioning the manner in which it was implemented and its potential impact on the region's stability.

Similarly, the Ayodhya verdict, while providing a legal resolution, also faced scrutiny from those who believed that it did not adequately address the historical injustices associated with the demolition of the Babri Masjid. The delicate balance struck by the Supreme Court aimed to reconcile legal principles with the imperatives of communal harmony.

Critics argue that the BJP's approach to these historical issues may polarize society along religious lines and undermine the principles of secularism. The party, however, asserts that its actions are driven by a commitment to justice, cultural preservation, and a vision of a unified India where diverse identities coexist harmoniously.

6.5 Lessons Learned and National Integration:

The BJP's handling of historical issues offers lessons on the complexities of national integration and identity in a diverse and pluralistic society. The party contends that its approach seeks to redress historical imbalances, restore cultural pride, and foster a sense of unity among diverse communities.

However, the challenges lie in striking a delicate balance between historical justice and communal harmony. The potential for social divisions and polarizations underscores the need for nuanced and inclusive approaches to historical issues, considering the sensitivities of all stakeholders.

6.6 Implications for the Future:

The resolutions of Article 370 and the Ayodhya dispute set important precedents for the BJP's governance philosophy. The party's willingness to confront historical issues head-on, coupled with its commitment to legal resolutions, reflects a proactive approach to addressing complex challenges.

Looking ahead, the implications of these historical resolutions for the BJP and India's political landscape are multifaceted. They shape the narratives of nationalism, religious identity, and historical justice, influencing the contours of political discourse and societal expectations.

The BJP's engagement with historical issues like Article 370 and the Ayodhya dispute reflects a dynamic approach to governance, navigating the complexities of India's diverse socio-political fabric. These historical chapters, marked by legal resolutions and cultural assertions, contribute to the evolving narrative of India's identity and the BJP's role in shaping the nation's destiny.

Chapter 7: Uniform Civil Code (UCC) and Citizenship Amendment Act (CAA): Navigating Legal Landscapes

In the expansive canvas of legal reforms and social discourse in India, two significant legislative initiatives have sparked intense debates and discussions – the Uniform Civil Code (UCC) and the Citizenship Amendment Act (CAA). This chapter unravels the nuances of these legislations, exploring their historical context, objectives, controversies, and the broader implications they hold for India's social fabric.

7.1 Uniform Civil Code (UCC): The Quest for Legal Uniformity

The concept of a Uniform Civil Code, as enshrined in Article 44 of the Indian Constitution Directive Principles, calls for a common set of laws governing personal matters, irrespective of religious affiliations. The idea is to replace the existing diverse set of personal laws based on religious practices with a singular code that would apply uniformly to all citizens of India.

The roots of the UCC debate lie in the broader pursuit of social justice, gender equality, and a desire to modernize legal frameworks. India, being a mosaic of diverse communities and religious traditions, has distinct personal laws for different communities – Hindu, Muslim, Christian, and others. Critics argue that this diversity often leads to gender-based discrimination, with each religious community having its own set of rules governing marriage, divorce, inheritance, and other personal matters.

The BJP, historically, has been a proponent of the UCC, arguing that a common civil code would contribute to national integration, gender justice, and the modernization of legal frameworks. The party contends that the UCC would bring uniformity, eliminate gender-based disparities, and uphold the principles of justice and equality enshrined in the Constitution.

However, the proposition of a Uniform Civil Code has been met with resistance from various quarters. Critics argue that imposing a uniform code may infringe upon the cultural and religious rights of communities, and any such reform should be implemented with sensitivity to diverse cultural practices.

7.2 Citizenship Amendment Act (CAA): Navigating Paths to Citizenship

The Citizenship Amendment Act, enacted in December 2019, became a focal point of national and international attention. The CAA provides a path to Indian citizenship for religious minorities (Hindus, Sikhs, Buddhists, Jains, Parsis, and Christians) from Afghanistan, Bangladesh, and Pakistan who arrived in India before December 31, 2014. It offers a mechanism for these communities, facing religious persecution in these countries, to seek refuge and, eventually, Indian citizenship.

The rationale behind the CAA lies in addressing the plight of persecuted religious minorities in neighbouring countries, particularly those belonging to non-Muslim communities. The BJP, in supporting the CAA, argues that it aligns with India's historical commitment to providing refuge to persecuted communities and is in line with the principles of humanitarianism.

Critics, however, express concerns about the exclusion of Muslims from the ambit of the CAA, viewing it as discriminatory and in violation of India's secular ethos. They argue that the act, when combined with the proposed National Register of Citizens (NRC), has the potential to render a significant number of Muslims stateless.

7.3 Historical Context and Controversies:

Both the UCC and the CAA have historical roots, embedded in the broader narratives of social justice, cultural diversity, and national identity. The UCC debate has its origins in the framing of the Indian Constitution, with the framers envisioning a future where citizens would be governed by a common set of laws irrespective of religious backgrounds.

The debates surrounding the UCC have intensified at various points in India's history, with successive governments hesitating to take decisive steps towards its implementation. The BJP's renewed push for the UCC reflects its commitment to a legal framework that transcends religious boundaries and fosters a sense of common citizenship.

On the other hand, the CAA's genesis lies in concerns about the persecution faced by religious minorities in neighbouring countries. The legislation aims to address the predicament of those who fled their countries due to religious persecution and sought refuge in India. However, the exclusion of Muslims and the potential linkage with the NRC led to widespread protests and criticisms.

Both legislations have been subjects of vehement debates, with supporters emphasising their potential to bring about social justice, national unity, and humanitarian relief, while opponents argue that they may lead to discrimination, polarisation, and challenges to the principles of secularism.

7.4 Gender Equality and Uniform Civil Code:

A significant aspect of the UCC debate revolves around the issue of gender justice. Critics of the existing personal laws argue that they often perpetuate gender-based discrimination. For instance, the Muslim Personal Law allows practices like triple talaq, which has faced criticism for being unfair to women.

Proponents of the UCC argue that a common code would eliminate discriminatory practices, provide equal rights to women in matters of marriage, divorce, and inheritance, and contribute to the broader goal of gender equality. The BJP, aligning with this perspective, emphasizes the importance of modernizing legal frameworks to reflect the principles of justice and equality enshrined in the Constitution.

However, critics caution against the imposition of a uniform code, emphasizing the need for sensitivity to diverse cultural practices. They argue that any reform in personal laws should involve a nuanced understanding of different communities' social structures and traditions.

7.5 Citizenship, Refuge, and Identity:

The CAA's objective of providing refuge to persecuted religious minorities from neighboring countries is rooted in India's historical tradition of offering sanctuary to those facing religious persecution. Supporters argue that it aligns with the principles of humanity, compassion, and India's commitment to protecting persecuted communities.

However, the exclusion of Muslims from the CAA's ambit has raised concerns about discrimination based on religion, potentially challenging India's secular fabric. Critics argue that the act, when combined with the NRC, may have unintended consequences, leading to the statelessness of a significant number of Muslims.

The debates surrounding the CAA intersect with broader discussions on identity, secularism, and India's commitment to religious pluralism. The BJP contends that the act is a humanitarian measure to address the specific challenges faced by certain religious communities, while critics argue that it may alter the foundational principles of Indian citizenship.

7.6 Political Perspectives and Public Opinion:

The UCC and the CAA have become significant political issues, shaping electoral narratives and party positions. The BJP, historically aligned with the ideological roots of the UCC and the principles behind the CAA, has been vocal in advocating for these legislations, presenting them as steps towards social justice, national integration, and humanitarian relief.

Opposition parties, while not uniformly against the principles behind these legislations, have raised concerns about the potential consequences and the need for inclusive and consultative approaches. The political discourse surrounding these issues reflects the broader ideological and identity-based fault lines within the Indian polity.

Public opinion on these legislations is diverse and often polarized. While some segments of society support the principles behind the UCC and the CAA, viewing them as steps towards modernization, justice, and humanitarianism, others express reservations about potential discrimination, the impact on cultural diversity, and the broader implications for India's secular identity.

7.7 Broader Implications for India's Social Fabric:

The UCC and the CAA represent attempts to navigate complex legal, social, and political landscapes, with broader implications for India's social fabric. The UCC, if implemented, could reshape personal laws, contributing to gender equality and a more uniform legal framework. However, the challenge lies in ensuring that reforms are inclusive, sensitive to diverse cultural practices, and do not infringe upon religious rights.

The CAA, with its focus on providing refuge to persecuted minorities, reflects India's commitment to humanitarian principles. However, the exclusion of Muslims raises questions about religious discrimination and the potential impact on India's secular ethos. The interplay between the CAA and the proposed NRC adds layers of complexity to the debates, requiring careful consideration of potential consequences.

7.8 The Way Forward: Balancing Unity and Diversity

Navigating the intricate landscapes of the UCC and the CAA requires a delicate balance between the quest for legal uniformity, social justice, and the preservation of cultural diversity. The challenges lie in crafting reforms that uphold constitutional principles, promote inclusivity, and address historical injustices without inadvertently fostering discrimination or polarizing society.

The BJP's commitment to the UCC and the CAA reflects a particular vision for India's future, emphasizing legal modernization, humanitarian relief, and a nuanced approach to social justice. However, the success of these initiatives lies in their ability to garner broad-based support, address concerns raised by critics, and ensure that they contribute positively to India's social fabric.

In conclusion, the UCC and the CAA represent attempts to navigate complex issues at the intersection of law, religion, and identity. The discussions surrounding these legislations encapsulate the broader challenges and opportunities inherent in India's journey towards a more inclusive, just, and harmonious society. The way forward involves thoughtful deliberation, inclusive dialogue, and a commitment to principles that balance unity with diversity.

Chapter 8: Social Welfare Initiatives: Transforming Lives, Fostering Inclusivity

In the realm of governance, the Bharatiya Janata Party (BJP) has embarked on a transformative journey, seeking to uplift the lives of the marginalized and foster inclusivity through a series of social welfare initiatives. This chapter explores the key initiatives undertaken by the BJP-led government, spanning education, healthcare, poverty alleviation, and empowerment programs, with a focus on their impact on diverse sections of society.

8.1 Education for All: Saakshar Bharat and Beti Bachao, Beti Padhao

Recognizing the pivotal role of education in empowering individuals and communities, the BJP has championed initiatives to enhance literacy and educational opportunities across the nation. The 'Saakshar Bharat' program, launched in 2009, aimed at promoting adult education and eradicating illiteracy, particularly among women.

Building on this foundation, the 'Beti Bachao, Beti Padhao' (Save the Daughter, Educate the Daughter) campaign, launched in 2015, focused on addressing gender-based discrimination in education and promoting the education of girls. The initiative aimed at changing mindsets, encouraging enrollment of girls in schools, and ensuring their holistic development.

The impact of these initiatives is evident in the increased literacy rates and the changing societal perception towards the education of girls. The focus on education not only empowers individuals but also contributes to broader socio-economic development.

8.2 Healthcare: Ayushman Bharat and Swachh Bharat Abhiyan

Healthcare has been a cornerstone of the BJP's social welfare agenda, with a commitment to ensuring affordable and accessible medical services for all. The 'Ayushman Bharat' program, launched in 2018, encompasses both the Pradhan Mantri Jan Arogya Yojana (PM-JAY) and the Health and Wellness Centres (HWCs). PM-JAY aims at providing health insurance coverage to vulnerable families, while HWCs focus on preventive and primary healthcare.

The ambitious 'Swachh Bharat Abhiyan' (Clean India Mission), launched in 2014, addresses the crucial link between sanitation and public health. The campaign emphasizes the construction of toilets, proper waste management, and the promotion of hygiene practices, contributing to a healthier and cleaner environment.

These healthcare initiatives underscore the BJP's commitment to ensuring that health services are not a privilege but a fundamental right. The emphasis on preventive healthcare aligns with a vision of building a robust healthcare ecosystem that addresses the diverse needs of the population.

8.3 Poverty Alleviation: Jan Dhan Yojana and Direct Benefit Transfer

Poverty alleviation has been a key focus area for the BJP-led government, with initiatives designed to provide financial inclusion and direct benefits to the economically disadvantaged. The 'Pradhan Mantri Jan Dhan Yojana' (PMJDY), launched in 2014, aimed at ensuring that every household has access to basic banking facilities, encouraging savings, and fostering financial literacy.

Complementing this, the 'Direct Benefit Transfer' (DBT) system seeks to streamline government subsidies and benefits by directly transferring funds to the bank accounts of beneficiaries. This prevents leakages, reduces corruption, and ensures that the intended beneficiaries receive the full benefits of welfare programs.

These poverty alleviation initiatives represent a paradigm shift in the approach to social welfare, emphasizing financial inclusion and empowerment. By providing individuals with the means to access and manage their financial resources, the BJP aims to break the cycle of poverty and create a more economically resilient society.

8.4 Empowerment Programs: Stand Up India and Pradhan Mantri Awas Yojana

Empowering marginalized communities and ensuring their participation in economic activities have been key objectives of the BJP's social welfare initiatives. 'Stand Up India,' launched in 2016, is a comprehensive program that facilitates bank loans for Scheduled Castes (SCs), Scheduled Tribes (STs), and women entrepreneurs to promote entrepreneurship and self-employment.

The 'Pradhan Mantri Awas Yojana' (PMAY), initiated in 2015, addresses the critical issue of housing for the urban and rural poor. The program aims at providing affordable housing to all by 2022, with a focus on creating a conducive environment for sustainable and inclusive urban development.

These empowerment programs are designed to break barriers and create avenues for the economic upliftment of historically marginalized communities. By fostering entrepreneurship and providing dignified housing, the BJP seeks to create a more equitable and inclusive society.

8.5 Skill Development: Skill India and Start-up India

Recognizing the evolving needs of the job market and the importance of skill development in fostering economic growth, the BJP has launched initiatives to enhance the employability of the youth. 'Skill India,' launched in 2015, focuses on providing vocational training and skill development to enable individuals to secure better employment opportunities.

In tandem with this, 'Start-up India,' launched in 2016, encourages entrepreneurship and innovation by providing a conducive ecosystem for start-ups. The initiative aims to create a culture of entrepreneurship, fostering job creation and economic growth.

These skill development initiatives reflect the BJP's commitment to preparing the workforce for the demands of the 21st-century economy.

By focusing on both employability and entrepreneurship, the programs contribute to building a skilled and dynamic workforce.

8.6 Social Inclusion and Tribal Welfare: Van Dhan Yojana and Eklavya Model Residential Schools

The BJP's commitment to social inclusion extends to the welfare of tribal communities, ensuring that they too reap the benefits of development. 'Van Dhan Yojana,' launched in 2018, seeks to empower tribal communities by providing them with skill development, value addition to forest produce, and market linkage opportunities.

The 'Eklavya Model Residential Schools,' initiated to provide quality education to tribal children, reflects the BJP's dedication to bridging the education gap between tribal and non-tribal communities. These residential schools offer a conducive learning environment, ensuring that tribal children have access to quality education.

These initiatives underline the BJP's commitment to ensuring that development reaches the farthest corners of the country, leaving no community behind. By focusing on the unique needs and challenges faced by tribal communities, the party aims to foster social equity and inclusivity.

8.7 Challenges and Future Directions:

While the BJP's social welfare initiatives have achieved notable successes, challenges persist. Implementation hurdles, ensuring the effective reach of programs to the last mile, and addressing the diverse needs of a vast population are ongoing challenges. Furthermore, a dynamic socio-economic landscape requires continuous adaptation and innovation in social welfare strategies.

The future of social welfare initiatives in India will require a holistic and integrated approach. Addressing the root causes of poverty, inequality, and marginalization, coupled with innovative policy frameworks, will be crucial. The BJP's commitment to social welfare remains integral to its vision of a prosperous and inclusive India.

8.8 Impact Assessment and Public Perception:

Assessing the impact of social welfare initiatives requires a nuanced understanding of the multifaceted challenges facing Indian society. While quantitative indicators such as improved literacy rates, healthcare coverage, and poverty reduction are crucial, qualitative aspects such as enhanced empowerment, social inclusion, and improved quality of life are equally significant.

Public perception of these initiatives plays a pivotal role in shaping their success. Continuous engagement with communities, addressing grievances, and incorporating feedback into policy revisions are essential for sustaining public support. The narrative around social welfare initiatives should reflect the tangible improvements in the lives of beneficiaries.

8.9 The Way Forward: Nurturing Inclusive Development

The BJP's social welfare initiatives stand as a testament to the party's commitment to inclusive development. As India navigates the complexities of a diverse and dynamic society, the way forward involves building on the successes of existing programs, addressing shortcomings, and innovating to meet evolving challenges.

A collaborative approach, involving partnerships with civil society, the private sector, and international organizations, can enhance the impact of social welfare initiatives. Additionally, leveraging technology for efficient implementation, data-driven decision-making, and ensuring transparency will be critical in achieving sustained and equitable development.

The BJP's social welfare initiatives reflect a vision of India where every citizen, regardless of socio-economic background, has the opportunity to lead a dignified and empowered life. By addressing the multifaceted challenges faced by diverse communities, the party endeavors to nurture a society that is not only economically resilient but socially inclusive, ensuring that the dividends of development reach every stratum of the population.

Chapter 9: Digital India and Technological Advancements: Bridging the Digital Divide

In the era of rapid technological evolution, the Bharatiya Janata Party (BJP) has championed the cause of digital empowerment and technological advancements through the ambitious 'Digital India' campaign. This chapter explores the multifaceted dimensions of Digital India, delving into its objectives, key initiatives, and the transformative impact of technological innovations on various sectors.

9.1 Digital India Campaign: Transforming Governance and Empowering Citizens

Launched in 2015, the 'Digital India' campaign is a comprehensive initiative that envisions the transformation of India into a digitally empowered society and knowledge economy. Rooted in the principles of inclusivity, accessibility, and efficiency, the campaign seeks to bridge the digital divide and bring the benefits of technology to every citizen.

- **Connecting Citizens:**

One of the central pillars of the Digital India campaign is the push for digital connectivity. The expansion of high-speed internet infrastructure and the BharatNet project aim to provide broadband connectivity to the remotest corners of the country. This connectivity not only facilitates access to information but also serves as a catalyst for economic and social development.

- **E-Governance and Service Delivery:**

Digital India emphasizes the digitization of government services, making them accessible to citizens through online platforms. Initiatives like the

National e-Governance Plan (NeGP) and the Digital Locker system streamline administrative processes, reduce paperwork, and enhance the efficiency of service delivery. The goal is to create a citizen-centric and transparent governance model.

- **Digital Literacy and Skill Development:**

Recognizing the importance of digital literacy in leveraging technological advancements, Digital India places a strong emphasis on skill development. Programs like Pradhan Mantri Gramin Digital Saksharta Abhiyan (PMGDISHA) aim to impart digital literacy skills to citizens, empowering them to participate in the digital economy.

- **Promoting Start-ups and Innovation:**

Digital India fosters an ecosystem conducive to innovation and entrepreneurship. Initiatives like 'Start-up India' provide a platform for young entrepreneurs to harness technology and contribute to economic growth. The campaign encourages the development of innovative solutions to address societal challenges.

9.2 Technological Innovations and Connectivity: Pioneering the Digital Revolution

- **BharatNet: Connecting the Unconnected**

At the heart of the Digital India campaign lies BharatNet, a transformative initiative aimed at laying a robust optical fiber network across rural and remote areas. By bridging the digital divide, BharatNet seeks to empower citizens with access to information, education, and economic opportunities. The project's completion is pivotal in ensuring that the benefits of the digital revolution are not confined to urban centers but extend to the grassroots.

- **Aadhaar: The Foundation of Digital Identity**

Aadhaar, India's unique biometric identification system, has emerged as a linchpin in the Digital India narrative. With over a billion enrollments, Aadhaar provides citizens with a secure and portable digital identity. It facilitates targeted service delivery, financial inclusion, and ensures that citizens can seamlessly access a myriad of government services.

- **Unified Payments Interface (UPI): Transforming Digital Transactions**

The introduction of UPI has revolutionized the landscape of digital transactions in India. A standardized and interoperable platform, UPI enables users to make instant and secure payments directly from their smartphones. The success of UPI reflects the growing acceptance and adoption of digital payment methods, contributing to the vision of a less-cash economy.

- **Swachh Bharat Mission (SBM) App: Harnessing Technology for Social Impact**

The Swachh Bharat Mission, focused on ensuring cleanliness and sanitation, leverages technology through the SBM app. Citizens can use the app to report cleanliness-related issues in their vicinity, fostering a collaborative approach to civic responsibility. This digitized feedback mechanism enhances the efficiency of the mission and promotes community participation.

- **GeM: Transforming Procurement through e-Marketplace**

Government e-Marketplace (GeM) is an innovative platform that facilitates transparent and efficient procurement by government agencies. Through GeM, vendors can register, showcase their products, and participate in e-bidding processes. The platform not only streamlines procurement but also enhances opportunities for small and medium enterprises (SMEs) to engage with government departments.

9.3 Transformative Impact on Sectors: Education, Healthcare, and Agriculture

- **Education: e-Learning and Digital Classrooms**

Digital India has revolutionized the education sector by promoting e-learning and digital classrooms. Initiatives like the SWAYAM platform provide access to a plethora of online courses, enabling students, especially in remote areas, to pursue education beyond traditional boundaries. The integration of technology in education enhances learning outcomes and prepares the youth for the digital economy.

- **Healthcare: Telemedicine and Health Information Systems**

The healthcare sector has witnessed a paradigm shift with the integration of technology. Telemedicine services bridge the gap between healthcare providers and patients in remote areas, ensuring timely medical consultations. Electronic Health Records (EHRs) streamline patient information management, improving healthcare delivery and facilitating data-driven policymaking.

- **Agriculture: e-NAM and Precision Farming**

In the agricultural landscape, Digital India has introduced e-NAM (National Agriculture Market), an online platform that connects agricultural produce markets, providing farmers with a wider market reach. Precision farming, enabled by technology, involves data-driven agricultural practices that optimize resource utilization and enhance crop yields. These digital interventions empower farmers with information and tools to make informed decisions.

9.4 Challenges and Opportunities: Balancing Connectivity with Cybersecurity

While Digital India has made remarkable strides, it faces challenges that necessitate careful navigation. Cybersecurity concerns, ensuring data privacy, and addressing the digital divide in remote areas are critical aspects that require sustained attention. Building a resilient digital infrastructure and fostering a cybersecurity ecosystem are imperative for the sustainable growth of the digital revolution.

The opportunities presented by emerging technologies such as artificial intelligence, blockchain, and the Internet of Things (IoT) hold the potential to further elevate India's digital landscape. Integrating these technologies into governance, healthcare, and education can unlock new avenues for innovation and efficiency.

9.5 Public Perception and Future Trajectory:

Public perception of Digital India is pivotal in shaping its trajectory. The widespread adoption of digital technologies, especially in rural areas, indicates the success of the campaign in reaching the masses. However, addressing concerns related to data security, digital literacy, and ensuring that the benefits are inclusive will be crucial for maintaining public trust.

The future trajectory of Digital India involves staying ahead of technological advancements, fostering research and development, and adapting to evolving digital trends. The integration of emerging technologies, coupled with robust cybersecurity measures, will play a key role in determining the sustainability and resilience of India's digital landscape.

9.6 The Way Forward: A Digitally Empowered India

As India continues its journey towards becoming a digitally empowered society, the way forward involves a holistic and collaborative approach. Strengthening digital infrastructure, enhancing cybersecurity measures, and ensuring that the benefits of technology reach every citizen are paramount.

The BJP's commitment to Digital India reflects a vision of an inclusive and technology-driven nation. By harnessing the transformative power of digital technologies, the party aims to not only bridge the urban-rural divide but also create a future where every citizen has the opportunity to participate in and benefit from the digital revolution. In navigating this trajectory, India stands poised to emerge as a global leader in the digital age.

Chapter 10: Infrastructure Development: Paving the Path to Progress

In the pursuit of holistic development, the Bharatiya Janata Party (BJP) has placed a significant emphasis on infrastructure development, recognizing it as a cornerstone for economic growth and societal progress. This chapter delves into the multifaceted dimensions of infrastructure development, exploring the initiatives undertaken by the BJP-led government in areas such as roads, railways, airports, and medical institutes.

10.1 Roads and Connectivity: Building the Backbone of Progress

- ### Pradhan Mantri Gram Sadak Yojana (PMGSY): Rural Connectivity Revolution

The Pradhan Mantri Gram Sadak Yojana, launched in 2000, is a transformative initiative aimed at connecting rural areas through all-weather roads. The program has played a pivotal role in enhancing accessibility, promoting economic activities, and empowering rural communities. By prioritizing connectivity, PMGSY has facilitated the integration of remote regions into the broader economic landscape.

- ### Bharatmala Pariyojana: Strengthening National Highways

The Bharatmala Pariyojana, unveiled in 2017, is an ambitious project aimed at improving the efficiency of freight and passenger movement across the country. The program focuses on the development of national highways, expressways, and economic corridors, enhancing connectivity and reducing travel time. Through Bharatmala, the BJP envisions a seamless road network that catalyzes economic growth and regional development.

- **Sagarmala Project: Boosting Coastal Connectivity**

Recognizing the potential of coastal regions in fostering trade and economic activities, the Sagarmala Project was initiated to develop a comprehensive port-led infrastructure network. By connecting ports with road and rail networks, Sagarmala aims to reduce logistics costs, enhance maritime trade, and unlock the economic potential of coastal areas. The project aligns with the BJP's vision of promoting balanced regional development.

- **Connectivity in Border Areas: Strategic Infrastructure Development**

Infrastructure development in border areas is of strategic importance for national security and regional stability. The BJP-led government has prioritized the construction of roads and bridges in border regions, ensuring better accessibility for defense forces and fostering economic development in remote areas. The focus on border connectivity reflects a commitment to safeguarding the nation's frontiers while promoting inclusive development.

10.2 Railways, Airports, and Medical Institutes: A Comprehensive Approach

- **Modernizing Railways: The Vision of New India**

Indian Railways, often referred to as the lifeline of the nation, has undergone significant modernization under the BJP-led government. Initiatives such as the Dedicated Freight Corridor (DFC) and the introduction of semi-high-speed trains like Vande Bharat Express aim to enhance the efficiency and capacity of railway transportation. The commitment to high-speed rail projects further underscores the vision of a modern, efficient, and sustainable railway network.

• Airports and Regional Connectivity: UDAN Scheme

The Ude Desh ka Aam Nagrik (UDAN) scheme, launched in 2016, focuses on enhancing regional connectivity by promoting affordable air travel. By connecting underserved and unserved airports, UDAN has not only made air travel accessible to a broader segment of the population but has also stimulated economic activities in smaller cities and towns. The expansion and modernization of airports contribute to the overall growth of the aviation sector.

• AIIMS and Medical Institutes: Advancing Healthcare Infrastructure

The establishment of All India Institutes of Medical Sciences (AIIMS) across various states reflects the BJP's commitment to upgrading healthcare infrastructure. AIIMS institutions serve as apex healthcare hubs, offering advanced medical services, research facilities, and medical education. This strategic investment in healthcare infrastructure aims to address regional imbalances and ensure that quality healthcare is accessible to all.

• Smart Cities Mission: Urban Infrastructure Revitalization

The Smart Cities Mission, launched in 2015, is a transformative initiative aimed at rejuvenating urban infrastructure. By integrating technology and sustainable practices, the mission seeks to enhance the quality of life in urban areas. The development of smart cities not only addresses urban challenges but also fosters innovation, economic growth, and efficient resource utilization.

- **Swachh Bharat Abhiyan: Sanitation and Urban Infrastructure**

While primarily focused on sanitation, the Swachh Bharat Abhiyan also encompasses the development of urban infrastructure. The construction of public toilets, waste management systems, and cleanliness drives contribute to the overall improvement of urban areas. The mission aligns with the broader vision of creating livable and sustainable urban environments.

10.3 Challenges and Opportunities: Sustainable Infrastructure for Future Generations

While the BJP-led government has made significant strides in infrastructure development, challenges persist. Sustainable and inclusive development requires overcoming issues such as environmental impact, funding constraints, and ensuring that the benefits reach all sections of society. Balancing the imperative for rapid development with environmental sustainability remains a critical consideration.

Opportunities abound for leveraging technology, public-private partnerships, and innovative financing models to address these challenges. The incorporation of smart technologies, renewable energy solutions, and community engagement can enhance the sustainability and resilience of infrastructure projects.

10.4 Public Perception and Future Trajectory:

Public perception plays a crucial role in shaping the success of infrastructure development initiatives. The widespread acceptance and appreciation of projects such as improved roads, efficient railways, and modernized airports indicate positive public sentiment. Addressing concerns related to environmental impact, displacement, and equitable distribution of benefits will be essential for maintaining public trust.

The future trajectory of infrastructure development involves a holistic and integrated approach. The BJP's commitment to creating world-class infrastructure necessitates continuous innovation, adaptive governance, and a proactive response to emerging challenges. As India aspires to be a global economic powerhouse, the role of robust and sustainable infrastructure becomes increasingly pivotal.

10.5 The Way Forward: A Visionary Approach to Development

In conclusion, infrastructure development stands as a testament to the BJP's visionary approach to nation-building. The commitment to creating a robust and sustainable infrastructure network reflects an understanding of its pivotal role in fostering economic growth, ensuring national security, and improving the quality of life for citizens. As India charts its course towards a future of prosperity and progress, the BJP's infrastructure development initiatives pave the way for a resilient and inclusive nation.

Chapter 11: Inclusivity and Outreach: Bridging Divides, Fostering Unity

In the pursuit of a harmonious and united India, the Bharatiya Janata Party (BJP) has championed initiatives focused on inclusivity and outreach. This chapter explores the party's endeavors to bridge regional, religious, and social divides, with a special focus on initiatives in South India, the North East, and education for Muslims.

11.1 Initiatives in South India and the North East: Nurturing Regional Unity

- **South India: A Tapestry of Cultures and Identities**

South India, with its rich cultural diversity and unique identity, has been a focal point for the BJP's efforts to foster regional unity. The party has recognized the importance of respecting and embracing the distinct cultural nuances of the southern states. Initiatives such as cultural festivals, language preservation programs, and economic development projects have been undertaken to strengthen the bond between the central government and the people of South India.

The establishment of the Chennai-Bengaluru Industrial Corridor and the development of infrastructure projects in the region are examples of the BJP's commitment to fostering economic growth and prosperity in South India. By addressing the region's specific needs and aspirations, the party aims to build a sense of inclusivity that transcends regional differences.

- **North East: Nurturing Connectivity and Development**

The North East, with its unique geographical and cultural landscape, has been a focus area for the BJP's inclusive development agenda. Recognizing the historical neglect of the region, the party has implemented infrastructure projects, connectivity initiatives, and cultural exchange programs to integrate the North East more closely with the rest of the country.

The 'Act East Policy,' which seeks to enhance economic and cultural ties with Southeast Asian nations, aligns with the BJP's vision of positioning the North East as a gateway to broader regional collaboration. The improvement of road and rail networks, along with the promotion of tourism, reflects the party's commitment to ensuring that the benefits of development reach every corner of the North East.

11.2 Education for Muslims: Empowering through Knowledge

• Empowering Through Education: A Vision of Inclusive Growth

Recognizing the importance of education as a tool for empowerment, the BJP-led government has undertaken initiatives to address educational disparities and promote inclusivity among Muslims. The focus is on providing quality education, skill development, and ensuring equal opportunities for Muslim students.

The 'Seekho Aur Kamao' (Learn and Earn) scheme, launched in 2013, is designed to provide vocational training and skill development to minority youth, including Muslims, to enhance their employability. By equipping individuals with skills aligned with market demands, the initiative aims to foster economic independence and bridge the gap in educational attainment.

• Scholarships and Financial Assistance: Breaking Barriers

To address financial barriers that may impede access to education, the BJP-led government has expanded scholarship programs for minority students, including those from the Muslim community. Initiatives such as the Pre-Matric and Post-Matric scholarships provide financial assistance to students at different educational levels. These programs are geared towards ensuring that financial constraints do not hinder the pursuit of academic excellence.

- ● **Madarsa Modernization: Integrating Traditional and Modern Education**

In an effort to bridge the gap between traditional Islamic education and mainstream academic curriculum, the BJP-led government has introduced the 'Scheme for Providing Quality Education in Madrasas' (SPQEM). The scheme aims to modernize and bring madrasa education into the mainstream, integrating subjects like mathematics, science, and social studies alongside religious studies. This approach is designed to provide students with a well-rounded education that aligns with contemporary academic standards.

- ● **Promoting Higher Education: Encouraging Aspirations**

The emphasis on higher education is a key aspect of the BJP's inclusive approach. Schemes such as the 'Maulana Azad National Fellowship for Minority Students' support minority students pursuing research-level studies. Additionally, efforts have been made to increase the presence of minority students, including those from the Muslim community, in prestigious institutions of higher learning. By encouraging aspirations and providing avenues for academic excellence, the BJP aims to ensure that no community is left behind in the pursuit of higher education.

11.3 Challenges and Opportunities: Navigating Complexities for Inclusive Growth

While the BJP's initiatives for inclusivity and outreach have made substantial strides, challenges persist. Ensuring effective implementation, addressing deep-rooted socio-economic disparities, and garnering community support for educational reforms are complex tasks. Navigating the intricate socio-cultural fabric requires a nuanced understanding of diverse communities' needs and aspirations.

Opportunities lie in leveraging technology, community engagement, and fostering partnerships with civil society organizations. By incorporating local perspectives, tailoring initiatives to regional contexts, and promoting dialogue, the BJP can enhance the impact of inclusivity and outreach programs.

11.4 Public Perception and Future Trajectory:

Public perception plays a pivotal role in determining the success of inclusivity and outreach. Positive reception and active participation from communities indicate the effectiveness of the BJP's efforts. However, building trust and ensuring sustained community engagement will be crucial for the long-term success of these initiatives.

The future trajectory involves a continuous commitment to inclusivity, listening to community feedback, and adapting policies to evolving needs. The BJP's vision for an inclusive and united India requires ongoing efforts to address the diverse challenges faced by different communities.

11.5 The Way Forward: A United and Inclusive India

In conclusion, the BJP's initiatives in South India, the North East, and education for Muslims underscore a commitment to building a united and inclusive nation. By recognizing and addressing regional and socio-economic disparities, the party endeavors to create a society where every individual, regardless of background or identity, has the opportunity to thrive. As India progresses on the path to inclusive growth, the BJP's vision of a united and harmonious nation stands as a guiding principle for the future.

Chapter 12: Looking Ahead: 2024 Elections Predictions

As the political landscape in India evolves, anticipation builds for the upcoming 2024 general elections. The Bharatiya Janata Party (BJP), with its multifaceted track record and strategic initiatives, stands poised for a significant electoral contest. This chapter delves into the landscape of Indian politics, analyzing key factors that may shape the outcome of the 2024 elections and providing predictions based on current trends and developments.

12.1 The Current Political Landscape: A Dynamic Scenario

● Economic Recovery and Development:

The performance of the Indian economy in the lead-up to the elections will likely play a pivotal role. A robust economic recovery, job creation, and effective management of inflation could bolster the BJP's electoral prospects. The implementation of key economic policies, infrastructure projects, and social welfare initiatives may contribute to the party's narrative of inclusive development.

● Pandemic Management and Healthcare:

The handling of the COVID-19 pandemic and the state of the healthcare system will be critical factors. Successful vaccination drives, effective pandemic management, and improvements in healthcare infrastructure could influence voters' perceptions of the government's ability to navigate crises. The BJP's response to public health challenges and its communication strategy will be closely scrutinized.

● Regional Dynamics:

Understanding and responding to regional dynamics will be crucial for the BJP's electoral strategy. The party's initiatives for South India and the North East, as discussed in previous chapters, may influence voter sentiment in these regions. Tailoring policies to address specific regional concerns and aspirations will be essential for building a diverse and inclusive electoral coalition.

• Social Welfare Initiatives:

The impact of social welfare initiatives on various segments of society will be a key factor in shaping voter perceptions. Successful implementation, public awareness, and effective communication of these initiatives will contribute to the BJP's narrative of governance that prioritizes the well-being of citizens.

• Digital India and Technology:

The role of technology in governance and its impact on various sectors, as discussed in Chapter 8, may resonate with a tech-savvy electorate. The BJP's initiatives in digitization, connectivity, and technological advancements could influence the voting choices of a population increasingly reliant on digital platforms for information and services.

12.2 Predictions and Scenarios: Assessing Potential Outcomes

• Scenario 1: Continued Popular Mandate

If the BJP successfully communicates its achievements in economic recovery, pandemic management, and social welfare, it could secure a continued popular mandate. Positive perceptions of the government's performance, combined with effective outreach and a united party strategy, may result in the BJP maintaining or even expanding its electoral footprint.

- **Scenario 2: Coalition Dynamics and Alliances**

The political landscape may witness the formation of strategic alliances and coalitions, with regional parties playing a crucial role. The BJP's ability to navigate coalition dynamics, build alliances, and address regional aspirations will be decisive. A coalition government could emerge if opposition parties form strong alliances to counterbalance the BJP's influence.

- **Scenario 3: Shifting Political Dynamics**

Unforeseen events, political developments, or shifts in public sentiment could significantly alter the electoral landscape. A dynamic and adaptive approach by the BJP to respond to emerging challenges or capitalize on opportunities will be crucial. Rapid adjustments to changing political dynamics may determine the party's success in navigating the uncertainties of the election season.

12.3 Challenges and Opportunities: Strategic Considerations for the BJP

- **Addressing Regional Concerns:**

To strengthen its electoral position, the BJP must continue addressing regional concerns and aspirations. Tailoring policies to specific regional needs, fostering dialogue with regional leaders, and ensuring effective representation will be essential for building a broad-based electoral coalition.

- **Communication and Narrative Building:**

Effective communication remains a cornerstone of political success. The BJP must continue to articulate its vision, achievements, and future plans in a manner that resonates with diverse segments of the electorate.

Clear and persuasive messaging will be critical in shaping public perceptions.

- **Responsive Governance:**

Responsive governance, characterized by the swift resolution of challenges, adaptability to evolving circumstances, and a commitment to addressing citizens' needs, will be paramount. Proactive measures to address emerging issues and a commitment to continuous improvement will enhance the BJP's image as a responsive and accountable government.

- **Youth and Urban Outreach:**

Given the demographic profile of India, with a significant youth population and increasing urbanization, the BJP must pay attention to the concerns and aspirations of urban and youth voters. Engaging with these segments through targeted policies, outreach programs, and digital communication channels will be vital.

12.4 Public Perception and Voter Sentiment: Navigating the Narrative

- **Trust and Credibility:**

Building and maintaining trust and credibility will be central to the BJP's electoral success. Transparent governance, accountability, and a commitment to ethical conduct will contribute to positive public perception. Addressing any concerns related to governance, policy implementation, or political conduct will be crucial.

- **Grassroots Connect:**

Ensuring a strong grassroots connection through effective party organisation, local leadership, and community engagement will be instrumental. The BJP's success in mobilizing support at the grassroots level will contribute to a groundswell of public sentiment in its favour.

- ● **Public Outreach and Participation:**

Encouraging public participation, feedback, and involvement in the political process will contribute to a sense of inclusivity. The BJP must continue its efforts to foster a participatory democracy, ensuring that citizens feel heard and represented in the political decision-making process.

12.5 The Way Forward: Navigating the Electoral Terrain

As India prepares for the 2024 general elections, the BJP stands at a critical juncture in its journey. The way forward involves a strategic and adaptive approach, emphasizing inclusive governance, effective communication, and responsiveness to the diverse needs of the electorate.

The BJP's ability to navigate the complexities of the political landscape, address regional dynamics, and build on its record of governance will determine its success in the 2024 elections. As the party continues its commitment to the vision of a prosperous and united India, the electoral terrain presents both challenges and opportunities that will shape the trajectory of Indian politics in the years to come.

Chapter 13: Challenges and Opportunities Ahead: Navigating the Future

As the Bharatiya Janata Party (BJP) charts its course for the future, a careful analysis of the challenges it faces and the opportunities that lie ahead becomes imperative. This chapter explores the multifaceted landscape of Indian politics, outlining key issues that need to be addressed and identifying avenues for sustained growth and success.

13.1 Issues to Address:

● **Socio-Economic Disparities:**

One of the central challenges that the BJP must grapple with is the persistent socio-economic disparities that exist across the country. While the government has implemented various social welfare programs, addressing the root causes of inequality requires sustained efforts. Tailoring policies to uplift marginalized communities, focusing on skill development, and creating opportunities for inclusive economic growth will be crucial.

● **Environmental Sustainability:**

Environmental concerns, including climate change, pollution, and ecological degradation, demand increased attention. Balancing economic development with environmental sustainability is a delicate task. The BJP needs to formulate and implement policies that promote sustainable practices, invest in renewable energy, and address the challenges posed by climate change. A proactive stance on environmental issues will resonate positively with a socially conscious electorate.

● **Healthcare Infrastructure:**

The ongoing COVID-19 pandemic has underscored the importance of a robust healthcare system. Strengthening healthcare infrastructure, ensuring access to quality medical services, and investing in research and development are critical aspects. The BJP's future agenda should include comprehensive healthcare reforms to enhance the country's preparedness for health crises and improve overall public health outcomes.

- **Technology and Digital Divide:**

While the BJP has made significant strides in promoting Digital India, addressing the digital divide remains a challenge. Ensuring that the benefits of technological advancements reach all segments of society, particularly in rural and remote areas, requires continued efforts. Bridging the digital gap will contribute to more inclusive development and economic participation.

13.2 Opportunities for Growth:

- **Innovation and Research:**

Encouraging innovation and research can propel India towards becoming a global leader in various sectors. The BJP can seize the opportunity to invest in research and development, foster a culture of innovation, and create an environment conducive to startups and entrepreneurship. Embracing cutting-edge technologies will not only drive economic growth but also enhance India's competitiveness on the global stage.

- **Education Revolution:**

A transformative education revolution can be a key driver of socio-economic development. The BJP can capitalize on the momentum generated by existing initiatives and further invest in education infrastructure, teacher training, and curriculum development.

Emphasizing skill-based education aligned with industry needs will empower the youth and prepare them for the challenges of a rapidly evolving job market.

● Foreign Relations and Global Partnerships:

As the world becomes increasingly interconnected, strategic foreign relations and global partnerships present significant opportunities. The BJP can leverage diplomatic ties to attract foreign investment, facilitate technology transfer, and collaborate on issues of global significance. Strengthening international cooperation can enhance India's standing on the global stage and open avenues for economic growth and technological advancements.

● Inclusive Governance:

Inclusivity in governance remains a potent opportunity for the BJP. The party can build on its track record of reaching out to diverse communities, addressing regional aspirations, and ensuring representation for all sections of society. A commitment to inclusive governance fosters a sense of belonging among citizens and strengthens the social fabric of the nation.

13.3 The Way Forward: A Visionary Approach to Governance

Navigating the challenges and harnessing the opportunities ahead requires a visionary approach to governance. The BJP can set a transformative agenda by adopting the following principles:

● Responsive and Agile Governance:

An agile and responsive governance model that can adapt to changing circumstances will be essential. Rapid responses to emerging challenges, efficient policy implementation, and a proactive approach to addressing citizen needs will strengthen the BJP's governance credentials.

- **People-Centric Policies:**

Prioritising policies that directly impact the lives of citizens is crucial. Whether it's healthcare, education, or economic development, the BJP can focus on people-centric initiatives that resonate with the aspirations and well-being of the diverse Indian population.

- **Collaboration and Consultation:**

Engaging in meaningful collaboration and consultation with stakeholders, including civil society, experts, and citizens, will enhance the effectiveness of governance. Building consensus on key issues, seeking diverse perspectives, and fostering a participatory approach will contribute to a more inclusive and democratic decision-making process.

- **Communication and Transparency:**

Transparent communication about government policies, achievements, and challenges is fundamental. The BJP can strengthen its relationship with the public by ensuring transparency in decision-making processes, providing regular updates, and actively addressing concerns through open communication channels.

In conclusion, the challenges and opportunities ahead present a dynamic landscape for the BJP. By addressing key issues, embracing transformative opportunities, and adopting a visionary approach to governance, the party can continue its journey towards building a prosperous, inclusive, and united India. The commitment to responsive, people-centric policies will be the guiding force as the BJP charts the way forward in the ever-evolving landscape of Indian politics.

Chapter 14: Conclusion: Reflecting on the BJP's Journey and India's Political Future

14.1 Summarizing the BJP's Journey:

The Bharatiya Janata Party's (BJP) journey from its inception to the present day has been marked by transformative leadership, strategic vision, and a commitment to building a New India. As we reflect on the party's trajectory, several key milestones and themes emerge, shaping its identity and impact on the nation.

- **Founding Principles and Early Leaders:**

The BJP, rooted in the principles of cultural nationalism and Hindutva, emerged as a political force in the post-independence era. Guided by leaders such as Shyama Prasad Mukherjee and Deendayal Upadhyaya, the party laid the foundation for its ideological framework. The articulation of a distinctive vision for India became integral to the BJP's identity.

- **Vision for India:**

The BJP's vision for India encompasses a holistic development agenda, emphasizing economic growth, national security, and social welfare. From the Atal Bihari Vajpayee era's 'India Shining' campaign to Narendra Modi's call for 'Sabka Saath, Sabka Vikas,' the party has consistently communicated a vision of progress, inclusivity, and unity.

- **Transformative Leaders:**

Leadership has been a driving force in the BJP's journey. The transformative leadership of individuals like Atal Bihari Vajpayee, who spearheaded economic reforms and conducted successful nuclear tests, and Narendra Modi, who brought a decisive and dynamic style of governance, has left an indelible mark on the party's legacy.

- **Inclusive Governance:**

The BJP's commitment to inclusive governance is evident in its policies and initiatives. From social welfare programs like Jan Dhan Yojana, Ujjwala Yojana, and Swachh Bharat Abhiyan to initiatives for regional development and minority education, the party has strived to address the diverse needs of the Indian population.

- **Economic and Infrastructure Development:**

Infrastructure development, economic reforms, and the 'Make in India' campaign have been key pillars of the BJP's agenda. Initiatives like GST, demonetization, and digital India underscore the party's focus on modernization, technological advancements, and economic growth.

- **National Security and Defense:**

A resolute stance on national security and defense has been central to the BJP's governance. From surgical strikes to the abrogation of Article 370 and the construction of the Ram Mandir, the party has demonstrated a firm commitment to safeguarding India's territorial integrity and cultural heritage.

- **Social Welfare Initiatives:**

The BJP's emphasis on social welfare is exemplified through schemes like Ayushman Bharat, Pradhan Mantri Awas Yojana, and the direct benefit transfer system. These initiatives aim to uplift the marginalized, provide healthcare access, and ensure housing for all, aligning with the party's vision of an inclusive society.

14.2 Reflections on India's Political Future:

As we look ahead to India's political future, the BJP stands at the crossroads of challenges and opportunities. The evolving political landscape and the aspirations of a dynamic and diverse population present a canvas for the party to paint a vision that resonates with the pulse of the nation.

• Political Landscape:

India's political landscape is characterized by its vast diversity, regional complexities, and a dynamic electorate. The BJP's ability to navigate these intricacies, address regional concerns, and forge strategic alliances will play a pivotal role in shaping its future electoral success.

• Changing Dynamics:

As societal norms evolve, demographics shift, and technology transforms communication, the BJP must adapt to changing dynamics. Engaging with the youth, leveraging digital platforms, and staying attuned to emerging issues will be imperative for maintaining political relevance.

• Inclusive Governance as a Guiding Principle:

Inclusivity in governance, a core principle for the BJP, will continue to be a guiding force. The party's commitment to addressing socio-economic disparities, ensuring regional representation, and fostering unity among diverse communities will be instrumental in shaping its future trajectory.

• Embracing Technological Advancements:

The rapid pace of technological advancements offers both challenges and opportunities. Embracing innovation, leveraging digital platforms for governance and communication, and ensuring that the benefits of technology reach all segments of society will be crucial for the BJP's future success.

- **Sustainable Development:**

As the world grapples with environmental challenges, the BJP has an opportunity to lead in sustainable development. Balancing economic growth with ecological responsibility, investing in renewable energy, and addressing climate change will align the party with global imperatives.

- **Strengthening Global Relations:**

In an interconnected world, fostering strong global relations and partnerships will enhance India's standing on the international stage. The BJP can leverage diplomatic ties to attract foreign investment, collaborate on research and development, and contribute to global problem-solving.

- **Responsive Governance in the Face of Uncertainties:**

The future is inherently uncertain, with unforeseen challenges and opportunities on the horizon. Responsive governance, characterized by adaptability, transparency, and a commitment to the welfare of citizens, will be the bedrock of the BJP's continued success.

14.3 The Way Forward:

As the BJP embarks on the journey ahead, it must carry forward the principles that have defined its legacy—transformative leadership, inclusive governance, and a vision for a prosperous and united India. By addressing challenges, embracing opportunities, and staying attuned to the evolving needs of the people, the BJP can continue to shape India's political landscape and contribute to the nation's progress. The journey ahead is a canvas awaiting the strokes of visionary leadership, and the BJP stands poised to paint a future that resonates with the aspirations of every Indian citizen.